BLADED EDGE BETWEEN

BLADED EDGE BETWEEN

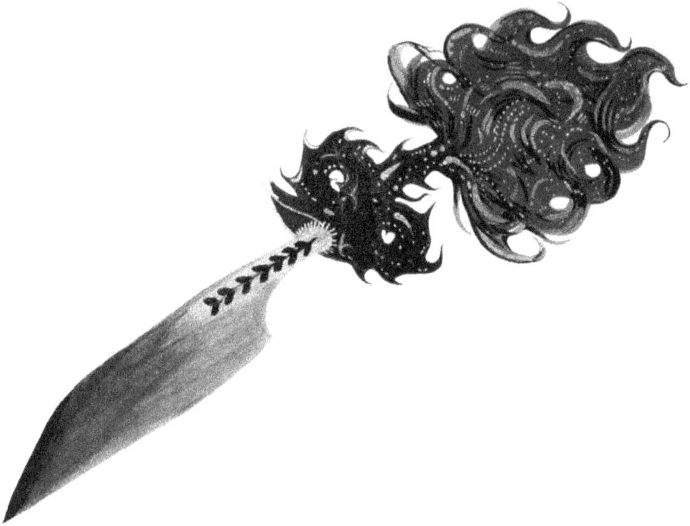

RUBY SINGH

Published by
Next Page Press
San Antonio, Texas
www.nextpage-press.com
© 2025 Ruby Singh. All rights reserved.

No part of this book may be used or reproduced in any manner without written permission from the publisher, except in context of reviews.

ISBN: 978-1-7366721-7-4
Library of Congress Control Number: 2025938675

Book team:
Laura Van Prooyen, *director and editor*
Hari Alluri, *editor*
Avery Letendre, *proofreader*
Amber Morena, *book designer*

Panjabi translation and script by Gurcharan Singh Sidhu
Cover and interior artwork by Sab Meynert

Contents

ALAAP | TAAL | RAAG
ਅਲਾਪ | ਤਾਲ | ਰਾਗ

    Five Rivers | 3 |

    A Boy | 5 |

    The Space Between | 6 |

    Sangeet: ਅਲਾਪ | 7 |

    Currency | 8 |

    Needle in the Sky | 9 |

    Today I Have Found (Aaj Rung Hai) ਆਜ ਰੰਗ ਹੈ | 10 |

    Sangeet: ਤਾਲ | 14 |

    Salt Water | 15 |

    Jhooti | 16 |

    Horizon | 18 |

    Sangeet: ਰਾਗ | 19 |

AROHI | AVROH | BANDISH
ਆਰੋਹੀ | ਅਵਰੋਹ | ਬੰਦਿਸ਼

Jhumar | 23 |

Signals | 24 |

Understand Death | 25 |

Sangeet: ਆਰੋਹੀ | 26 |

Let This In | 27 |

In This World of Night | 28 |

When We Were Children | 29 |

Sangeet: ਅਵਰੋਹ | 30 |

Beyond the Fourth Wall | 31 |

And They Still Burn | 32 |

Beyond the Second Wall | 33 |

I Was Mothered By | 34 |

Beyond the First Wall | 36 |

Sangeet: ਬੰਦਿਸ਼ | 37 |

JHALA | RELA | KHALI
ਝਾਲ | ਰੇਲਾ | ਖਾਲੀ

Crow's Nest |41|

The Clouds Stood as Giants |42|

Tears Weave Us Together |43|

Sangeet: ਝਾਲ |45|

Initiation |46|

The Women in My Family |47|

Overflowing |49|

Ma |50|

Sangeet: ਰੇਲਾ |52|

Ride the Bench |53|

Sunken Grey Roads |54|

Magnetic Storm |55|

Sleepless |56|

A Jubilation of Emptiness | Khali ਖਾਲੀ |57|

Sangeet: ਖਾਲੀ aka Hidden Track |59|

| TIHAI |
| ਤਿਹਾਈ |

    A Thousand Sons | 63 |

    I Am Holding You | 64 |

    A Beacon for the Other Side | 65 |

    A Beacon from the Other Side | 67 |

    Open the Talisman | 68 |

    Darkness Has a Source as Surely as Light Does | 69 |

    Sangeet: ਤਿਹਾਈ | 70 |

    Between Ribs & Courage | 71 |

    Stick to My Ribs | 72 |

    Listen for Her Prayers' Return | 73 |

Acknowledgements and Gratitude | 75 |
About The Author | 77 |

ALAAP | TAAL | RAAG

ਅਲਾਪ | ਤਾਲ | ਰਾਗ

Five Rivers

I wash myself in the ghats of your memories
My being submerged in your depths
3 times to honour the blood running through my veins
once for earth
once for sky
once for life

5 rivers stretching in all directions
A blood partition of 2:3
sikhing the horizon

These currents guide and thrash
determined and stubborn
coerce my body until spirit finds meaning

No matter where the fault lines
the undertow still believes

You of Sutlej
Daughters of Beas and Chenab

Sons of Ravi and Jhelum
students and disciples
of the many names

wear your heart
in your eyes
:
Behold

A Boy

A boy once believed light was a ladder and climbed
to the moon just for a picnic of white sugar on white bread
slowly trading away his smile for a lifelong mercury leach

A boy who believed that summoning dragons was the only way
to reach mountain's temple
A boy who believed hand-feeding your loved ones was how you celebrate life
A boy who believed leaving a light on would keep the demons at bay

Because the silence of his family's suffering offered no other explanation,
for 6 years he believed he killed his mother,
thought he had stopped her heart and stole the joy from his father's eyes

Although he believed the thunder of your voice was an ancient god
quaking fear out of his eyes and revealing encoded warnings,
no matter how much the table would shake, he believed he could
find sanctuary under your rib cage

I was that boy who believed a creek could become the river styx
luring me back, my boots filling, growing heavier with the water of after-life
hoping that a full plunge in the current would carry my spirit to you

The Space Between

clove, ginger and cinnamon spells to awaken the day
    we can only hold our dreams for so long
      so we imbued what we could hold with their essence
      laid to bare in earth and water, palm and finger tip

I could only hold these dreams for so long
    before they vanished from my desperate arms
    laid bare in earth and water, palm and finger tip
    the cloud dissolves to offer light—the last tangerine kiss of sun

before they vanished from my desperate arms
    I lost the memories of what your touch did to my spine
    the cloud dissolves to offer light—the last tangerine kiss of sun
    but the taste is of void, unsweetened

I lost the memories of what your touch did to my spine
    so I imbue what I can hold of your essence
    sweeten the taste of the void:
    clove, ginger and cinnamon spells to awaken the day

Sangeet: ਅਲਾਪ

Hold my body together
Music tuned to the vibration
of these cells of ancestry
Woven understanding immediate
Lata's voice takes me back

Currency

Clouds gather melodies strike shits coming down down down drown limitless abyss dreams swim centuries futures coil open time condensed time served steely brass valves shift alternate notes ¼ moans ¼ loans catch grips currency pulses echoes silent through skin rattle cages stir in   us   a   sanctuary

Needle in the Sky

I've been searching a world over but I never thought to look right here
I wait for your tongue to breach air, whisper something I need to hear

> The smallest hairs of our bodies are built for this intimacy
> you can be delicate with your approach, I am standing just here

These arms eternally stretched like arbutus reach and hold the sky
a mother tongue with no vessel, caress what you hear

> Time condensed in the husk of fog, all gravities spiral,
> head over healing us, leaving us here

> Lend your ear to the needle in the sky,
> the clouds are composing hymns for you to hear

> The song of always brings Ruby closer
> dropping love tracks encoded in the wind, tune in right here

Today I Have Found (Aaj Rung Hai) ਆਜ ਰੰਗ ਹੈ

after Amir Khusro & Kaifi Azmi

I only know you through another's eyes
someone touched by the tides of your grace
that still pours through like the salt waters of our past

    always with us
    all ways a part of us

They tell me stories of your heart
they still carry like crimson lanterns in their chests
a blaze that keeps each of your loved ones warm

    jhalthe jhalthe o mera sath
    jhalthe jhalthe

    ਜਲਦੇ ਜਲਦੇ ਉਹ ਮੇਰੇ ਨਾਲ
    ਜਲਦੇ ਜਲਦੇ

It has lit my path by extension, illuminated every future possibility
of what we would have always become

4 sons in a galaxy of your care

    jhalthe jhalthe o meri raat
    jhalthe jhalthe

    ਜਲਦੇ ਜਲਦੇ ਉਹ ਮੇਰੀ ਰਾਤ
    ਜਲਦੇ ਜਲਦੇ

a momentum for constellations to spread across these spirits
like a current of air that gives rise to wings
like a gravity that guides these stars

    jhalthe jhalthe o mera saath
    jhalthe jhalthe

    ਜਲਦੇ ਜਲਦੇ ਉਹ ਮੇਰੇ ਨਾਲ
    ਜਲਦੇ ਜਲਦੇ

You, weaver, threading through infinite veils
life cycles death, death give way for life
seed plant fruit soil seed plant fruit
soil seed

    always with us
    all ways a part of us

The immortal formless, the I am mortal form
you are the myth in my blood
building worlds inside worlds

    always with us
    all ways a part of us

They tell me I have your eyes and lips
I've stared at this photo in my room for years
and still can't see it

    Main to jab dekhun moray sung hai ri,
    Aaj rung hai ri Maan rung hai ri

ਮੈ ਜਦੋ ਵੀ ਦੇਖਾਂ ਤੂੰ ਮੇਰੇ ਨਾਲ ਹੈਂ
ਆਜ ਰੰਗ ਹੈ ਮੇਰੀ ਮਾਂ ਰੰਗ ਹੈ ਨੀਂ

A love like yours that knows no distance, entangled in every all things
resonates and joins the nada brahma
A love that can fill a son who is older now than you ever would be

Main to jab yaad kahroon moray sung hai ri
Aaj rung hai ri Maan rung hai ri

ਮੈਂ ਜਦੋਂ ਵੀ ਦੇਖਾਂ ਤੂੰ ਮੇਰੇ ਨਾਲ ਹੈਂ
ਆਜ ਰੰਗ ਹੈ ਮੇਰੀ ਮਾਂ ਰੰਗ ਹੈ ਨੀਂ

Today I have found the divine is glowing
in the vibrant colours of your remembrance

    always with us

    jhalthe jhalthe
    ਜਲਦੇ ਜਲਦੇ

    all ways a part of us

Sangeet: ਤਾਲ

Keep turning and folding until the water becomes clear
Fold and press on rock with creek water
Turn, turn, turn and push
The silky fabric between her hands and mine

Salt Water

She took my hand and we dove into the mystery of her eyes. Both she and I knew it would be the last time we'd see each other, there we bathed in a wisdom folded over and into lifetimes. She had lived by the cycles of seasons, deep breathing before the sun would rise

Both she and I knew it would be the last time we'd see each other. Sending prayers to a family tree of which she was the seed. She had lived by the cycles of seasons deep breathing before the sun would rise. I held her weathered feet in my hands callused and curved, worn, wise

Sending prayers to a family tree of which she was the seed, born of a banyan, roots that carry grace from sky to earth. I held her weathered feet in my hands callused and curved. Worn and wise, ageless stories written in the folds of her skin—

born of a banyan, roots that carry grace from sky to earth. Tears began to swell and fall, I kissed the salt water of my ancestors' ageless stories, written in the folds of her skin. She took my hand and we dove into the mystery of her eyes

Jhooti

Every time I move my skin gets pulled tighter
the collapse of shoulder into tendon into rib into memory
the folding over of emotion into control into escape

My origami heart gets confused about his shape
his grief brings out the truest colours of our skin
every time I move my skin gets pulled tighter

Topographical maps of saffron and indigo truths
that might lead him to where she was torn from this world
the folding over of emotion into control into escape

But time is a relative that can compress in men
lend days to where a panicked breath used to live
every time I move my skin gets pulled tighter

In my language mohabbat ki jhooti kahaani pey roya
so why would ours be any different
the folding over of emotion into control into escape

She once gave me a home where love is in the frame
knowing this might at least prepare me for the pining hollows
every time I move my skin gets pulled tighter
the folding over of emotion into control into escape

Horizon

seed to sparrow | light to water | caught in time amber
streak sky | smoke in ash | paper skin, no edge to air

the clouds whisper | these wings bring stories | risen from iridescent shells
tongue to tree limb | searching for light | my grandmother's bones

nourish that which comes after | tilt the horizon for days | and still the circle
shows itself the way | the path is under our feet dear one | let your lungs expand

be filled with all these offerings | hold and be held | curve into her light
like refractions in water | illuminate the constellations | pining for your eyes

Sangeet: ਰਾਗ

The corners, grip them to return the shape
shake side to side, elbow grease now to restore
to remind the cloth of its duty to her body

AROHI | AVROH | BANDISH
ਆਰੋਹੀ | ਅਵਰੋਹ | ਬੰਦਿਸ਼

Jhumar

Plow the field, sow the seed,
watch the growth, harvest
and celebrate

Witness the circle, invoke all of creation

The past kneels for the present,
the present dances for our future
ਝੂਮਰ

Signals

A heart at rest
beats only to send
signals across the air

These two eardrums
in time, sharing relations
to tell the tales that spirit enters

They pulse and echo
silent through this skin, rattle
cages, stir this in us:

a sanctuary for here.
A dawn may flicker

knowing, dear one, that life
lays in front of us and love

it is always inside, rest easy

Understand Death

I came as song
Tongue curve to shape air into lung

The wings in my throat take flight
I came as a fist folded in the shape of my heart

I came as a descendant of the moon
4th son of a first brother

Wanted daughter of the oldest sister
Calling myself back to the sky

on the night that I was born

Sangeet: ਆਰੋਹੀ

Exhale water to sky *Sa Re Ga Pa Ma*
A 3-year-old wrist flip of memories
Fine myst on face gathering air, gulabi
dupatta body plumes under cloud and over heart

Let This In

The handlebars' first grip
without training wheels, a blood knuckle belief
a scraped knee, the road rash
pebbles picked from left palm, right elbow, chin
then gripping again, refusing to walk

In This World of Night

ਦਿਲ ਦਾ ਦੀਵਾ
ਤੂੰ ਚੁਰਾ ਲਿਆ
ਹੁਣ ਕੀ ਕਰੀਏ
ਅਸੀਂ ਹਨੇਰੇ ਵਿੱਚ ਗੁੰਮ ਹੋ ਗਏ

ਲੱਭਦੇ ਲੱਭਦੇ
ਸਾਰੀ ਜ਼ਿੰਦਗੀ ਹਨੇਰੇ ਵਿੱਚ ਖੋ ਗਏ
ਹੁਣ ਕੀ ਕਰੀਏ
ਅਸੀਂ ਹਨੇਰੇ ਵਿੱਚ ਗੁੰਮ ਹੋ ਗਏ

ਤਾਰੇ ਤੇ ਚੰਦ ਸਾਰੇ ਛੁਪ ਗਏ
ਕੋਈ ਸੂਰਜ ਦੀ ਚਮਕ ਨੀ ਦੇਖ ਸਕਦੇ
ਕੀ ਕਰੀਏ
ਅਸੀਂ ਹਨੇਰੇ ਵਿੱਚ ਗੁੰਮ ਹੋ ਗਏ

ਕੀ ਕਰੀਏ

Dhil da diva
Tu chura liya
Hun ki khariye
Asi hanaray vich gumm ho gaye

Labhday Labhday
Sari zindagi haneray vich kho gaye
Hun ki khariye
Asi hanaray vich gumm ho gaye

Taray te chand sare chhup gaye
Koi suraj di chamak ni dekh sakdhe
Hun ki khariye
Asi hanaray vich gumm ho gaye

Hun ki khariye

When We Were Children

we would hang our hopes on the moon before closing our eyes
and watch them rise with the sun the next day

we built fantasies out of everything
from the Sasquatch who guarded the gates of the cemetery

to the water sprites who would pull my brother in
fill his rubber boots and send him down the river

I give thanks to Tim Kasner who saved him, even twice
swinging a fishing rod over one shoulder and a motorbike over the other

back to our trailer, the fortress we were always looking to escape
the great dragon steaming at the edge of combustion

there was a reason to cry over spilled milk
but always our bedroom window, a hatch,

a passage to where the golden light
still draws out our laughter

Sangeet: ਅਵਰੋਹ

Ni Da Pa Re Sa
The sinking cloth horizontal then belly
The flip the wrist the water drops again, the repetition

Beyond the Fourth Wall

entangled with Adrienne Rich

I know you are reading this

out loud because your voice will learn to reach the edges of any room you're put in
including that one person at the back of this empty theatre

because music notes play tricks on your mind and
terikita dum terikita dum terikita dum makes so much more sense

nestling your small understandings into your father's ribcage
while Peter Mansbridge's voice from the National seems to be the only one he can listen to

because it acts as a distraction from the nightmares waiting for you
1, 2, freddy's coming for you
3, 4, better lock your door
keep your eyes on the page so the demented shadows on the wall can't get you

I know you're reading this
because when you're reading this you are not as alone with your own thoughts
there's at least both of us until . . .

And They Still Burn

White knuckles on hot flames
Offering to Mars
Scar's pride open before
Salve has time to heal

Deafening echoes
Absorb the canyon
Left in these lungs
No space to breathe

Drowning in the ashes
Of a pale comparison

Tooth through tongue
I taste combustible mercury

Beyond the Second Wall

entangled with Adrienne Rich

I know you are reading this

next to a thousand scrolls of backlit distractions, opinions, grams and books
measured against each other, measured against this poem

because you are stuck in these walls like these books are stuck in your shelves
wondering if you will ever be able to throw off your covers and stretch your spine

under a lamp light that is a beacon for safety, a lighthouse that can keep
the smell of alcohol and anger at bay from over your right shoulder

while silver laden feathers press their way out
blades may finally give you the perspective you've been waiting for

I Was Mothered By

the whisper of morning prayers
under breath and over lips

the incense that lingered in the air
and the charcoal under my eyes

the bucket bath of infinite play
the exfoliating of the love placed inside me

a jewel forged by your gravity
time taken and given

fists folding and pushing turquoise skies
the myst that graced my little body

a parachute for our play
into the warm summers of lester's creek

the kneading and rolling
the open flame, the flip, the rise and fall

the generosity of your fingertips
guiding the taste of our ancestors

the many limbed goddess reached out
for the child in me

Beyond the First Wall
entangled with Adrienne Rich

I know you are reading this

tumbling through tall grass looking for the pictures that might lie in here
palm pressed to page to hold yourself open to possibility

at the edge of a playground with roped off jungle gyms
and hazard tape on the swings

with a desk laying on its side and the wrong lord's prayer forced onto your tongue
in a fake leather jacket that gives you skin in this game

under cedar bows next to the glowing light of the fire
the sound of the river mixing with the blood on your drum

Sangeet: ਬੰਦਿਸ਼

Ni Re Sa Ga Pa Re Sa
part memory part photograph, her vibrance
water being, life giver, ancestral creek
waterfall of children sleep in the pools of her being
her swollen body in a hospital bed
25 sense to send your child's sight away

JHALA | RELA | KHALI
ਝਾਲ | ਰੇਲਾ | ਖਾਲੀ

Crow's Nest

You protect your young as you hunt others
precise and without remorse. These streets

on stolen land, laden with petals. I don't mean to trespass.
you carry my thoughts to wonder and I forget every step

is an invasion. I catch a small glimpse
out from your side eyes, a threat. I curl to my right

and feathers emerge from my skin. I shift back and talons
emerge from my heart. This ribcage bursts open

transforming into wings, my voice turns to ash
from the sun I swallowed. My corvid wake,

darlings I want none to go hungry
in this palace of branch and wire. I have placed offerings

just for your young. My friends
there's no need to divebomb. I only want a closer glimpse

at your onyx feathers, how they refract light,
how they defy the gravity of spectrum.

The Clouds Stood as Giants

Watching my kin play
each of them choosing favourites
each of them gambling on who would burst with laughter next

Catch, release and soar
each of them defying gravity in their own way
bringing wings to cherub cheeks

Barefoot to blades of grass
a mother's knowing allows them room to grow
each of them held by the earth's understanding

From stubbed toe to scratched knee
each of them finding knowledge in skin
replaced hip to swollen disc

Their spirit has found the full spectrum
finding time waits for everyone to fall
fall into spring, into each other

Tears Weave Us Together

Across this digital stream
I feel you
the anger   the hurt   the love   the joy
the opening   the tender
that awaits when someone is truly witnessing

all of you

shifting moment to monument

Even when next is mystery
in the fluorescent corners of the hospital, our laughter
even with her feeding hands pushed to another wing

She still flies

Freedom in the toothy grin of knowing
that this isn't the last we will see of each other

Next to your fire
the eternal slips effortlessly into our lives
deep sighs. Dearest
this time we don't say goodbye

When flesh fails we still reach
through the zeros and the one

ੴ

Sangeet: ਭਾਲ

This one: Crowsnest
This one: Gumty
This one: Blairmore
This one: Ludhiana
Desh, ghar, Lembrook Falls, Frank Slide, pind

This one in the snow, the wonder in her eyes,
the cancer a snowflake none of us has noticed

Initiation

a golden light pours from the heavens
into her chalice, the initiation is open

her hands fold comfort into my effort to understand
what separation is, the remedy and the reminder

folding cotton over blood birth and skin
2 lungs 1 breath an origin, the softened sound

enters my ears slowly as if snowflakes were falling and melting
the biophony, hold me close like the stars always

have, they've scribed stories before time's curve
had reached our understanding, *there now, there,*

*gentle, recognize this: rhythm through skin remember
who you are*, I can feel the creases lining her hands

wrap around me, a blanket of memories to be stored
for another time, we mend, before the ascendant ascends

The Women in My Family

after Ellen Bass

The women in my family
Toil hour under hour weaving fabric and spices
Into the hearts of our tongues and backs
Mortar and pestle cardamom until it stirs

Toiling hour under hour, weaving fabric and spices
Into our dreams, at our waking
Mix water and wheat, knead and compress
Mortar and pestle cardamom until it stirs

Our dreams to wake
Flat bread over open flames
Mortar and pestle cardamom until it stirs
Place it tenderly into our mouths

Flat bread over open flames
Before they would think to feed themselves
Place it tenderly into our mouths
Use their voice and flesh as shields

Before they would think to feed themselves
Against the open palm and closed fist inferno of rage
Use their voice and flesh as shields
Against the combustion of broken dreams and loss

Against the open palm and closed fist inferno of rage
Coiling their limbs and torso's around our small bodies
Against the combustion of broken dreams and loss
Creating cocoons from which we will emerge

Coiling their limbs and torsos around our small bodies
Into the hearts of our tongues and backs
Creating cocoons from which we will emerge:
The women in my family

Overflowing

*I cannot contain this
this vessel is overflowing
a thousand cups have been put at its feet
and still it pours over
spilling into earth
remember dear ones
my love has flooded this land
feel me beneath your feet*

Ma

Half a life ago you wondered if the sacrifice was worth it
To cradle these broken hearts that you didn't know
To feed a child's wounds with your hands
They might learn what the love of a mother might taste like again

To cradle these broken hearts that you didn't know
You offered blood, skin, cloth and shelter from the storm
They might learn what the love of a mother might taste like again
Would you pass the selfish inquisition of the grieving child?

You offered blood, skin, cloth and shelter from the storm
Their desperate tongues only knew how to lash or stay silent
Would you pass the selfish inquisition of the grieving child?
You wondered if in time you would coax a kindness out of their eyes

Their desperate tongues only knew how to lash or stay silent
Sorrow had built a tower and the only window to look out had made you the enemy
You wondered if in time you would coax a kindness out of their eyes
You wondered if the child would ever stop calling you unti

Sorrow had built a tower and the only window to look out had made you the enemy
2 syllables that could break 4 chambers into a family of 6
You wondered if the child would ever stop calling you unti
Still there was no lumber for the ladder you needed no grip on the icy edges of their ribs

2 syllables that could break 4 chambers into a family of 6
To feed a child's wounds with your hands
A thawing on the icy edges of their ribs, a ladder you made by climbing
Two lifetimes later we would know the sacrifice was worth it

Sangeet: ਦੋਲਾ

A surrounding of women, ready to step up,
the child on one lap and all of them at once

Though one hand slipped another was always there
with too much ginger in the saag
with too much spice for a child's tongue
always fresh roti and dahi to mend the hurt

Ride the Bench

I can hear the sounds now, sole stretched across floor. The drumming of hollow air in skin, the pivots, the yelling from the sidelines. I grew in the shadow of 3 brothers, who would become a 5-point star, the triangle offense. A dream of 23 lifting childhood from folded socks to shining light, but no crossover for grace, no Jordans for lift. Just this adrenaline darting my eyes back and forth. A sneaker squeaks for the shift of direction, the screen set to free another's guard. Reach for leather and board, outlet to relieve the pressure. Fall to floor and pick yourself up, get back on defence. Hands out wide and active strain to reach all edges of the room. Confusion and duress. Shame is Mr. Stewart claiming, "You're nothing like your brother. Man up!" Benched pride: shame is being told, "sit down!" and sitting, because I do everything in my power to prove him wrong—pivot, crossed over, bounce, pass me by: this pit growing in my stomach tells me he's right. I slid further down the bench until I was finally out of sight. This is what I would do with the spectre of absence: place palms over knees, trace torso to face what I wanted to stay hidden—I would sacrifice tendon, meniscus and grief for a hollow belonging, not knowing I would soon ghost skin in another game.

Sunken Grey Roads

In the washed-out underbelly of what you said last night
I feel your shallow bleached eyes
a vermillion haunt

These burnt marigold off-ramps of when it's too much,
crossing into the borderlands of us

Perhaps this is the time to breathe diamonds,
to yield to oncoming versions, these disfigured pathways

Perhaps this is the coiled time when I
roll up my broken serpent synapses

Escalator my carnelian blood
up these crumbling stairs—

I escher my way back to you

Magnetic Storm

During a geomagnetic storm the auroral zone will expand to lower latitudes and dance with the spirits when the music is right. The charged particles originate in the magnetosphere and solar wind and are directed by the earth's magnetic field. It is important that a temporary magnetic connection be established between the field lines of the solar wind and those of the magnetosphere, by a process known as magnetic reconnection. When this happens the whole sky dances and everyone wakes and goes outside in bare feet and sees in the sky an image of the ones they love. Sound is a form of energy that moves through air, water, and other matter, in waves of pressure. When a dear one is drawing closer the temporal lobe becomes extremely sensitive, and the world begins to emit musical compositions, these sound waves crash directly into both hearts.

Sleepless

Lay dark / waiting night / seduce eyelids
Shadows move / whispering cars / 4 am still
Take me / time stares / facing broken
Loss Again / my unlit match still

Night-born / my corner / seven hollows / my skull
Fill them / salt water / pull me, undertow still
Playing fire / burnt gate / escape towards the leaving
Invisible steps chase midnight / no relief still

A Jubilation of Emptiness | Khali ਖਾਲੀ

after Dr. Karan Barad

nothing is free of ghosts
spectral realm get away
with something for nothing
pairs rapidly coming into out of
a phantom non:exist dance

    on the bladed edge the between
    no determinate words are spoken
    I.m.|.possibility non.|.existence
    only a speaking silence

we are not in the void but of
    :
    a lively tension
    threaded through the silence orienting

scales, ragas ਰਾਾ, whimpers, whines, alaap ਅਲਾਪ, shabaad ਸ਼ਬਦ, ghazals ਗ਼ਜ਼ਲ, pitches, mantraa ਮੰਤਰ, syncopations, shruti ਸ਼ਰੁਤੀ, sirens, blasts, bhajan ਭਜਨ, sighs, kirtan ਕੀਰਤਨ, baani ਬਾਣੀ, sangha ਤਸੰਗਤ , melody, taal ਤਾਲ, tempos, hip hop, pentatonic, gheet ਗੀਤ, dhrupad ਧਰੁਪਦ, lehera ਲੈਹਰਾ, tihai ਤਹਿਾਈ, sum ਸਮ,

khali ਖਾਲੀ

:

ready to erupt
simultaneously crosscut crossfade disruption
dispersing a symphony

when I think for a minute that there are no
material effects of yearning
the blank page teems
with desire traces every

inscription, symbol, word, book, library, punctuation mark, vowel, diagram, scribble, graphic, letter, design, story, myth, joke, poem, equation, script, inkblot, spell

:

conjure toward expression
nothing is free of ghosts

Sangeet: ਖਾਲੀ aka Hidden Track

Naada in the Brahma blurs the lines
The taste of childhood memories
Rotten tooth from sugar sandwiches
A late-night thief of bleached jewels

| TIHAI |
| ਤਿਹਾਈ |

A Thousand Sons

would suffer the eternal
darkness to illuminate
a path to your shelter

I Am Holding You

at least what's left of you in this cage these ribs

ache and this is my only hope of reaching you

I need to let you know so much but this ink is running

dry my lips you alone comfort this lonely soul I no longer know

what day or month it is my only timeline runs from where we left

each other to when we may meet again don't worry

I have the stars to keep me company but only to reflect

you illuminating a path atop the deepest of these treacherous

waters I am reaching for you, I am reaching to find solace

in my imagination where you reign

sovereign over any breach in this body—I am breathing

for you, I am breathing—any distance from this raft to your shore

A Beacon for the Other Side

Dear One,

You have been missed in this world

The joy bell you struck
when the hour was at its darkest

The corner mouth conjuring of your ways
when the rest of humanity felt lost
curling into the comfort of your laughter

In a world of porcupine quills
I wonder what your touch would feel like again
to origami into your outstretched arms

Folding into the feeling of home
held like clouds hold water like gravity holds an ocean

Only you could cast this panic to a burnt out star
visible from the other side of the planet

I could disappear from my longings, from my trespasses
if only I could catch your eyes with mine again
the air quality was always best there

Our conversation like perfume
intoxicating with an open invitation

I know you are being loved
by whatever star cluster you're visiting
please send out a beacon when the time is right

A Beacon from the Other Side

*my edges have lost themselves
each branch doused in this tide buoyant with air*

*salt water has baptized every corner
taking me under, over, around and through*

*panic removed from my lungs
an expanse, a comfort, a kick, a glide—*

*I learned to breathe deep in shallow waters
calmer still in the depths*

*I shift to hold someone else
bring myself back to earth*

*I shift, touch sky, a shift
keeps me coming back*

a condensation cycle of spirit

Open the Talisman

This week I open the talisman to see what was inside
Cries wept from the corner of this universe

The exaltation of long-lost relatives filled the air
Tears went for their casual stroll

To awaken the threat of not loving enough
Not caring enough for generations to come

What could one's arms hold if not the sky
Atlas burrowed into all our shoulders

Together (I miss you) we could lift everything
Hold up a universe as offering

Darkness Has a Source as Surely as Light Does

step into: step into:
mystery where the imaginations lay dormant in the slumber of night
void, the elixir of nothingness finding those spaces
in between

(a moon shadow dance with our love)
(a hand holding free fall with the infinite intimate)

hello oldest, truest friend
you've had me before my father could name me
and you'll have me after a thousand names are given

step into return:
the hollow, the nothing, the needless, the anointed

Sangeet: ਤਿਹਾਈ

The passing of the child from the mother to the bhua,
Teri kita thum: him sitting on the floor between them,
Teri kita thum: they stand on either side, clang together
Teri kita thum: hands dangled towards him
Sum: handheld.

Between Ribs & Courage

We have always been the descendants of the citrine hallow
filtering between the branches of knowing cedar and imagining winds
guiding lights of the mirror calling itself back to self

Extending palms holding the spine between ribs and courage
lifting what's needed and letting the weight settle
into what gravity will hold for you

We have always been the boat adrift on a shadow filled sea
our mast pointing towards the home of our ancestors
the reflection always runs true and straight through

Bio illuminated lanterns of the great uncoiling
the tethered ends of a ruby dress that has been whirling in ecstasy
before memory gave you a name
the grandmothering of prayer

We have always been the bare foot on the dusty path
tracing the lines etched by the many and known to the few
dot to dot drawing constellations
between the movement of our hearts

Stick to My Ribs

Light ripples soft through the trees, greet this day, a baptism for the woken breath, and I remember how we sit, incanting the scripts that have rippled the air for 500 years. Our kin expand past horizon, and my eyes are lifted by the prasad of the people, blessed by lightning, carried by earth, rubber and air to my tongue. Offer a kindness, there is room in the failure to speak only love today. There's room to try and remember her love. Tending the soil of grieving bones and mourning tendon, gravity continues to support me, my leaning, underpin for the pining. What faded memory of a satellite mind takes away can be found in a sweetness that can only be collected by wings. The way my lips are the same shape and can curve around the same words hers did. Cyclical time means we are always reaching for each other through web and crystal, fingertip, and garden.

Listen for Her Prayers' Return

before Isana

The seed feeds the dreams she has for your return
The garden feeds the seed, the flower feeds the garden's return

After all look we create a recognition of spectrum
A prism sits as a reminder behind your iris's return

In each footprint lies a thousand generations of struggle
This is not your first step or your last dance's return

As kin we can dance millennia around millennia
Slip through starry clusters, your light's return

They put wings in your chest so you could soar
Remember when you told them you wanted to return

The first breath rushes in and hits a child as a surprise
This breath that all your ancestors have breathed for your return

Belly to forearm, head curved into elbow
Their arms hold you just right for your return

Let your streams draw these signs of love as oceans
Behind your eyelids uncontrollable weeping, the cracks return

Leave some perspective to sit over your left shoulder
Push through soft crown's return

Breathe in sandalwood as the yellow sun begins to shower
Their corner of that blue marble with life's return

Acknowledgements and Gratitude

Sidhu Clan / Dhaliwal Clan / Dhillon Clan / Sekhon Clan / Laura June Albert, nothing is possible without your love and support. Rajinder Kaur Sidhu, Harjinder Kaur Sidhu, Nachhattar Kaur Dhaliwal and all the women in my family, thank you for your tireless care, patience and love. Gurcharan Singh Sidhu: a father's hand for a mother tongue. Margaret Isana Kaur Kendall Peña, Sara Kendell, Vanessa Peña, Jarrett Martineau, Tiffany Ayalik, August "Aku" Okaliq Ayalik-Martineau, Khari Wendell McClelland , Katherine Moriarty, Honey Rose McClelland, Poet McClelland, Kim Haxton, The Albert Clan, Paul Finlay, Tarun Nayar, Johanna Robertson, Marika Swan, Sennen Kathryn Sietcher, LJ Amsterdam, Preeti Kaur Dhaliwal, Bhupinder Dhaliwal, The Graveley Towers, Holly Eccleston, Harsha Walia, Harjap Grewal, Melina Miyowapan Laboucan Massimo, Vanessa Richards, Nadia Chaney, the GG's, Buoys!, Mark Voenesch, Michael Datura, Merlin Sheldrake, Erin Robinsong, Cosmo Sheldrake, Flora Wallace, Darrell Stables, Karma Leroux, Cecily Nicholson, Arthur Flowers, Cynthia Dewi Oka, Jillian Christmas, Faisal Mohyuddin, Tanya Tawida Evanson, Seema Reza and the Community Building Artworks team. Next Page Press for believing in this work, Laura Van Prooyen for your care and vision, Amber Morena for your cunning designs. Hari Alluri for the guiding light that saw this collection to fruition. Sab Meynert for your transporting artwork. Canada Council of the Arts, BC Arts Council, Lobe Studio, Deer Lake Residency, The McLoughlin Gardens Residency, The Banff Centre.

"Between Ribs and Courage" was in the compilation *We Were Not Alone* by CBAW and "Listen for Her Prayers Return" are lyrics that appear in Polyphonic Garden and Vox.Infold II

"A Jubilation of Emptiness | Khali ਖਾਲੀ" appeared in *Polyphonic Garden.*

About The Author

Ruby Singh is an award-winning poet, interdisciplinary artist, and educator based on the unceded territories of the xʷməθkʷəy̓əm, Sḵwx̱wú7mesh, and səl̓ílwətaʔɬ/Selilwitulh Nations (Vancouver, BC). His creative practice moves between poetry, music, photography, and film, weaving mythos, ecology, justice, and fantasy into vivid, boundary-crossing works.

Celebrated for his innovative voice, Singh has been honored with a Lieutenant Governor's Jubilee Award for excellence in Art and Music, multiple Jessie and Leo award nominations, a Juno nomination, and WCMA awards for both Global Music Artist and Electronic/Dance Artist of the Year. His expansive projects—from the a cappella constellation *Vox.Infold* to the sufi hip hop of *Jhalaak*—echo the spirit of his book of poems *Bladed Edge Between*: forging portals between worlds and singing through the thresholds of transformation. Singh believes in art's ability to reimagine futures, to repurpose aesthetic freedoms toward civil and environmental justice.

www.ingramcontent.com/pod-product-compliance
Lightning Source LLC
Chambersburg PA
CBHW081157070526
44583CB00021B/2889